JOSEPH HAYDN

TRUMPET CONCERTO

E♭ major/Es-Dur/ Mi♭ majeur
Hob. VIIe:1

Edited by
Hans Ferdinand Redlich

Ernst Eulenburg Ltd

London · Mainz · Madrid · New York · Paris · Prague · Tokyo · Toronto · Zürich

CONTENTS

Ernst Eulenburg Ltd
48 Great Marlborough Street
London W1F 7BB

PREFACE

Haydn's trumpet concerto must have caused some considerable astonishment at its premiere; the solo instrument confronted the audience with an entirely new soundscape never previously imagined. Such a phenomenon was due partly to Haydn's composition, but also to an innovation in instrumental construction. In the 1790s the Viennese trumpeter Anton Weidinger – after more than 20 years' experiment – introduced a trumpet that because of its technology as a keyed instrument afforded completely new ways of playing. Previously it had only been possible to perform the natural tone series on the trumpet; now, thanks to Weidinger's technological improvements the complete chromatic scale was available to the player. The new Eflat trumpet did, however, have one deficiency: the dullness of the sound quality. This drawback would only be remedied with the introduction of the valve trumpet in 1813. But with this further innovation, the significance of Weidinger's achievement would also be eclipsed.

Haydn, in his trumpet concerto, did, however, erect a lasting musical monument to Weidinger's achievements. Haydn had returned in 1796 from his extraordinarily successful second trip to England only a few months before Weidinger approached him with his new instrument and the request for a first composition to exploit its musical potential. The new technology and the compositional challenges associated with it seem to have awakened Haydn's interest. Thus he started work to create a solo concerto that would exploit to the full the musical possibilities of the keyed trumpet: cantabile elements could now determine its musical course instead of the three-note calls especially familiar in the trumpet repertory until then. In his concerto Haydn now naturally incorporates previously impossible parts of the scale in the low register of the instrument, and there seem to be no limits to the instrument's flexibility in chromatic passages.

The new technical achievements are apparent at the beginning of the *Allegro*. Following the orchestral introduction the solo trumpet (b37ff) introduces a diatonic scale passage placed very low in its register, the realization of which would previously have been unrealistic. The first movement of the concerto – in sonata form – progresses monothematically, at first with typical trumpet fanfare motifs, but followed by a contrasting cantabile passage. The development – in C minor – impresses not least because of its fast semiquaver runs culminating in a high D flat (b110) followed almost immediately by a descent to the lowest note of the movement B flat (b117), such an extreme of register being hitherto unplayable. The extended leaps in the reprise outline the available tonal space before renewed semiquaver figuration exploits the new-found technical ease afforded by the instrument. The descending chromatic course leads to the cadenza and the brief closing coda.

The second movement begins with a cantabile melody whose opening is reminiscent of the Emperor's Hymn composed only a few months before. The *Andante* is shaped as a three-part lied form, the middle section of which would have impressed its first audience especially because of its modulation to C flat major; until this time, such a key would have been completely out of range for brass players.

In the final movement Haydn effectively displays the assets of the new instrument in a favourable light, not least thanks to the successively brilliant runs each surpassing the other. However, a recollection of the original signaling function of the trumpet is not overlooked with the fanfare-like sounds of the *Allegro* allowing those origins to be recognized within the rondo-structure.

Despite its maturity the work belatedly received its premiere four years after its composition, on 28 March 1800 as part of a benefit concert by the trumpeter Weidinger. Even after its premiere the work failed to establish itself in the concerto repertory. More than a century had to pass before the work met with a sustained success and could finally join the most popular of Haydn's works.

Sandra Borzikowski
Translation: Margit McCorkle

VORWORT

Haydns Trompetenkonzert muss bei der Uraufführung absolutes Erstaunen verursacht haben, war das Publikum doch gerade mit gänzlich neuen, noch nie gehörten Klangmöglichkeiten des Soloinstruments konfrontiert worden. Die Einzigartigkeit des Ereignisses war zum einen Haydns Komposition zu verdanken, zum anderen aber auch einer Innovation auf dem Gebiet des Instrumentenbaus. In den 1790er Jahren hatte der Wiener Hoftrompeter Anton Weidinger – nach mehr als 20 Jahren andauernden Bemühungen – schließlich eine Trompete vorgestellt, die auf Grund ihrer Klappentechnik vollkommen neue Spielweisen erlaubte. War es den alten Instrumenten bisher lediglich möglich die Naturtonreihe wiederzugeben, so konnte sich der Musiker bei seinem Spiel nun fast ausnahmslos der gesamten chromatischen Skala bedienen und erstmals annähernd unbegrenzt jegliche melodische Vorgabe realisieren. Ein Defizit hatte die neue Trompete in Es jedoch: Die neue Klappentechnik ließ sich zunächst nur zu Lasten der Klangqualität umsetzen. Erst die Einführung der Ventiltrompete im Jahr 1813 sollte diesen letzten Makel noch aus dem Weg räumen. Doch damit verblasste auch die Bedeutung von Weidingers Erfindung.

Ein bleibendes musikalisches Denkmal setzte jedoch Jospeh Haydn diesem Instrument, für das er eigens sein Trompetenkonzert in Es-Dur komponierte. Haydn war erst einige Monate zuvor von seiner außerordentlich erfolgreichen zweiten Englandreise aus London zurückgekehrt, als Weidinger im Jahr 1796 mit seinem neuen Instrument und der Bitte um eine erste Komposition für dieses an ihn herangetreten war. Die neue Technik und die damit verbundenen kompositorischen Herausforderungen scheinen das Interesse Haydns geweckt zu haben. So begab er sich ans Werk, um ein Solokonzert zu schaffen, das alle Möglichkeiten der Klappentrompete ausschöpft: Kantable Elemente anstelle der bis dahin besonders geläufigen Dreiklangsmelodik bestimmen nun den musikalischen Verlauf. Zuvor unmögliche Tonleiterausschnitte in den tiefen Lagen des Instruments baut Haydn nun ganz selbstverständlich in seine Komposition ein, und auch der Flexibilät bei chromatischen Läufen scheint keine Grenzen gesetzt zu sein.

Schon zu Beginn des Allegro zeigen sich die neuen technischen Errungenschaften. Nach der orchestralen Einleitung wartet die Trompete mit einem für ihre Verhältnisse recht tief angelegten diatonischen Skalenausschnitt (T. 37ff.) auf, dessen Realisation bis zu diesem Zeitpunkt jenseits des Vorstellbaren lag. Monothematisch – zunächst mit den für die Trompete so typischen Fanfarenklängen, die aber bereits unmittelbar darauf mit einer kantablen Passage in Kontrast treten – schreitet der als Sonatenform konzipierte erste Satz des Konzerts voran. Die in c-Moll gehaltene Durchführung beeindruckt nicht zuletzt mit ihren raschen Sechzehntelläufen, die in einem vorläufigen Spitzenton (T. 110) gipfeln, um gleich darauf abermals den tiefsten, noch kurze Zeit zuvor unspielbaren Ton des Satzes anzusteuern (T. 117). Auch in der Reprise demonstrieren ausladende Sprünge den verfügbaren Tonraum bevor erneute Sechzehntelbewegungen mit scheinbarer Leichtigkeit ausgekostet werden. Der abwärts geführte chromatische Gang leitet im Anschluss zur Kadenz und der abschließenden knappen Coda über.

Der zweite Satz wird von einer kantablen Melodie eröffnet, deren erste Töne eine Art Reminiszenz an die nur wenige Monate zuvor komponierte Kaiserhymne darzustellen scheinen. Das Andante wurde von Haydn als dreiteilige Liedform gestaltet, deren Mittelteil auf Grund seiner Modulation nach Ces-Dur wohl besonders beeindruckte, schien diese Tonart bis zu diesem Zeitpunkt für die Blechbläser doch noch völlig außer Reichweite.

Effektvoll rückt Haydn auch im finalen dritten Satz die Vorzüge des neuen Instruments ins rechte Licht, nicht zuletzt die brillanten Läufe scheinen mitunter das bereits Gehörte noch zu übertreffen. Doch auch eine Rückbesinnung auf die ursprüngliche Signalfunktion der Trompete ist nicht zu übersehen. Die fanfarenartigen Klänge des in Form eines Rondos gehaltenen Allegros lassen diese Wurzeln erkennen.

Trotz seiner Ausgereiftheit sollte das Werk erst vier Jahre nach seiner Komposition, am 28. März 1800, im Rahmen eines Benefizkonzertes des Trompeters Weidinger zum ersten Mal in der Öffentlichkeit erklingen. Und auch nach seiner Uraufführung konnte sich das Werk nicht etablieren. Weit mehr als 100 Jahre mussten vergehen bis es einen nachhaltigen Erfolg erzielen und sich schließlich in die beliebtesten Kompositionen Haydns einreihen konnte.

Sandra Borzikowski

TRUMPET CONCERTO

Joseph Haydn
(1732–1809)
Hob. VIIe: 1

Edited by Hans Ferdinand Redlich

Fl.
Ob.
Fg.
Cor. (Es)
Tr. (Es)
Timp.
Tr. solo (Es)
Vl.
Vla.
B.
p
f
20
1.
Vcl.

Fl.
Ob.
Fg.
Cor. (Es)
Tr. (Es)
Timp.
Tr. solo (Es)
Vl.
Vla.
B.
a2
f
Bassi

30
Fl.
Ob.
1.
a2
Fg.
Cor.
(Es)
Tr.
(Es)
Timp.
Tr. solo
(Es)
Vl.
Vla.
B.
Solo
f
p

Fl.
Ob.
Fg.
Cor. (Es)
Tr. (Es)
Timp.
Tr. solo (Es)
Vl.
Vla.
B.
40
p
a2
f
tr

Fl.
Ob.
Fg.
Cor. (Es)
Tr. (Es)
Timp.
Tr. solo (Es)
Vl.
Vla.
B.
50
60
a2
1.
2.
tr
f
p

Fl.
Ob.
Fg.
Cor.
(Es)
Tr.
(Es)
Timp.
Tr. solo
(Es)
Vl.
Vla.
B.
70
a 2
f
p

80
Fl.
Ob.
Fg.
Cor. (Es)
Tr. (Es)
Timp.
Tr. solo (Es)
Vl.
Vla.
B.

90
Fl.
Ob.
Fg.
Cor. (Es)
Tr. (Es)
Timp.
Tr. solo (Es)
Vl.
Vla.
B.
Vcl.
1.
Bassi

100
Fl.
Ob.
Fg.
Cor. (Es)
Tr. (Es)
Timp.
Tr. solo (Es)
Vl.
Vla.
B.
a 2
1.
2.
p
f

110
Fl.
Ob.
Fg.
Cor. (Es)
Tr. (Es)
Timp.
Tr. solo (Es)
Vl.
Vla.
B.
1.
a 2
p
1.
p
120
pp

130
Fl.
Ob.
Fg.
Cor. (Es)
Tr. (Es)
Timp.
Tr. solo (Es)
Vl.
Vla.
B.
a 2
1.
p
f
tr

140
Fl.
Ob.
Fg.
Cor. (Es)
Tr. (Es)
Timp.
Tr. solo (Es)
Vl.
Vla.
B.
1.
a2

150
Fl.
Ob.
Fg.
Cor. (Es)
Tr. (Es)
Timp.
Tr. solo (Es)
Vl.
Vla.
B.
a2
tr
f
p

Fl.
Ob.
Fg.
Cor. (Es)
Tr. (Es)
Timp.
Tr. solo (Es)
Vl.
Vla.
B.
1.
p
160
a2
f
Bassi

Fl.
Ob.
Fg.
Cor. (Es)
Tr. (Es)
Timp.
Tr. solo (Es)
Vl.
Vla.
B.
170

II.

Andante

Solo

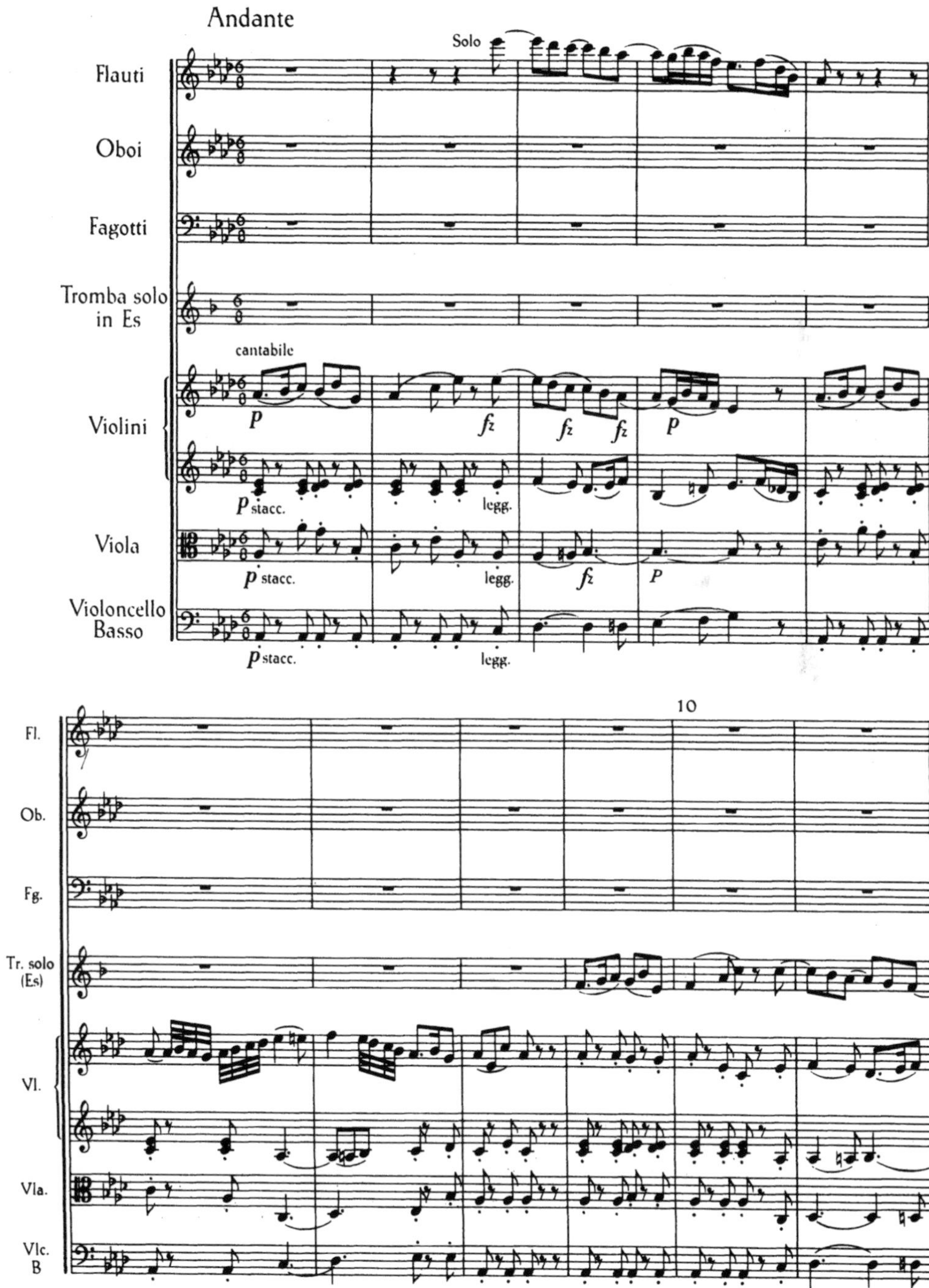
Flauti
Oboi
Fagotti
Tromba solo in Es
cantabile
Violini
p
fz
p
p stacc.
legg.
Viola
p stacc.
legg.
fz
P
Violoncello Basso
p stacc.
legg.
10
Fl.
Ob.
Fg.
Tr. solo (Es)
Vl.
Vla.
Vlc. B

Fl.
Ob.
Fg.
Tr. solo (Es)
Vl.
Vla.
Vlc. B.
(tenuto)
20

30
Fl.
Ob.
Fg.
Tr. solo
(Es)
Vl.
Vla.
Vlc.
B.
fz
p

Fl.
Ob.
Fg.
Tr. solo
(Es)
Vl.
Vla.
Vlc.
B.

40
Fl.
Ob.
Fg.
Tr. solo
(Es)
Vl.
Vla.
Vlc.
B.
fz
fz
fz
50

III.
Allegro
Flauti
Oboi
Fagotti
2 Corni in Es
2 Trombe in Es
Timpani in Es. B.
Violini
Viola
Violoncello Basso
10
p
Fl.
Ob.
Fg.
Cor. (Es)
Tr. (Es)
Timp.
Vl.
Vla.
Vlc. B.
a2
20
f

Fl.
Ob.
Fg.
Cor. (Es)
Tr. (Es)
Timp.
Tr. solo (Es)
Vl.
Vla.
Vlc. B.
30
Tutti

40
Fl.
Ob.
Fg.
Cor. (Es)
Tr. (Es)
Timp.
Tr. solo (Es)
Vl.
Vla.
Vlc. B.
50
Fl.
Ob.
Fg.
Cor. (Es)
Tr. (Es)
Timp.
Tr. solo (Es)
Vl.
p
p
Vla.
Vlc. B.

60
Fl.
Ob.
Fg.
Cor. (Es)
Tr. (Es)
Timp.
Tr. solo (Es)
Vl.
Vla.
Vlc. B.
p
pizz.
f
arco

70
Fl.
Ob.
Fg.
Cor.
(Es)
Tr.
(Es)
Timp.
Tr. solo
(Es)
Vl.
Vla.
Vlc.
B.
p
80
pizz.
arco

90
Fl.
Ob.
Fg.
Cor.
(Es)
p
Tr. solo
(Es)
Vl.
Vla.
Vlc.
B.
100
f
a2
p

110
Fl.
Ob.
Fg.
Cor. (Es)
Tr. (Es)
Timp.
Tr. solo (Es)
Vl.
Vla.
Vlc. B.
120
1.

130
Fl.
Ob.
Fg.
Cor.
(Es)
Tr.
(Es)
Timp.
Tr. solo
(Es)
Vl.
Vla.
Vlc.
B.
140
a2
1.
pizz.

150
Fl.
Ob.
1.
p
Fg.
Cor. (Es)
Tr. (Es)
Tr. solo (Es)
Vl.
fp
p
Vla.
arco
Vlc. B.
pizz.
160
Fl.
Ob.
f
a2
Fg.
f
Cor. (Es)
Tr. (Es)
Tr. solo (Es)
Vl.
f
f
Vla.
arco
Vlc. B.
p
f

170
Fl.
Ob.
Fg.
Cor. (Es)
Tr. (Es)
Tr. solo (Es)
Vl.
Vla.
Vlc. B.
180
Timp.
pizz.

190
Fl.
Ob.
Fg.
Cor. (Es)
Tr. (Es)
Timp.
Tr. solo (Es)
Vl.
Vla.
Vlc. B.
a2
f
arco
200
p
1.

Fl.
Ob.
Fg.
Cor. (Es)
Tr. (Es)
Timp.
Tr. solo (Es)
Vl.
Vla.
Vlc. B.
Vcl.
210
220
a 2
1.
Bassi
tr

230
Fl.
Ob.
Fg.
Cor.
(Es)
Tr. solo
(Es)
Vl.
Vla.
Vlc.
B.
pizz.
240
arco
1.
p
f
sfz

250
Fl.
Ob.
a2
Fg.
Cor.
(Es)
Tr.
(Es)
Timp.
Tr. solo
(Es)
Vl.
Vla.
Vlc.
B.
260
270

280
Fl.
Ob.
Fg.
Cor. (Es)
Tr. (Es)
Timp.
Tr. solo (Es)
Vl.
Vla.
Vlc. B.
mf
p
cresc.
a2
290
f
ff